DATE DUE

Ambulances

By Hal Rogers

The Child's World® Inc. ◆ Eden Prairie, Minnesota

Published by The Child's World®, Inc.
7081 W. 192 Ave.
Eden Prairie, MN 55346

Design and Production:
The Creative Spark, San Juan Capistrano, CA

Photos: © 1998 David M. Budd Photography

Library of Congress Cataloging-in-Publication Data

Rogers, Hal 1966-
      Ambulances / by Hal Rogers.
         p. cm.
         Includes index.
      Summary: Describes the parts of an ambulance, how it operates,
and the work it does.
        ISBN 1-56766-655-8 (lib. reinforced : alk. paper)
        1. Ambulances—Juvenile literature. 2. Emergency medical
services—Juvenile literature. [1. Ambulances.] I. Title.
     TL235.8.R64 1999
     629.222'34—dc21
                                               99-26590
                                                CIP

Contents

On the Job

On the job, an ambulance takes sick or injured people to the hospital. It is a big truck that can travel very quickly.

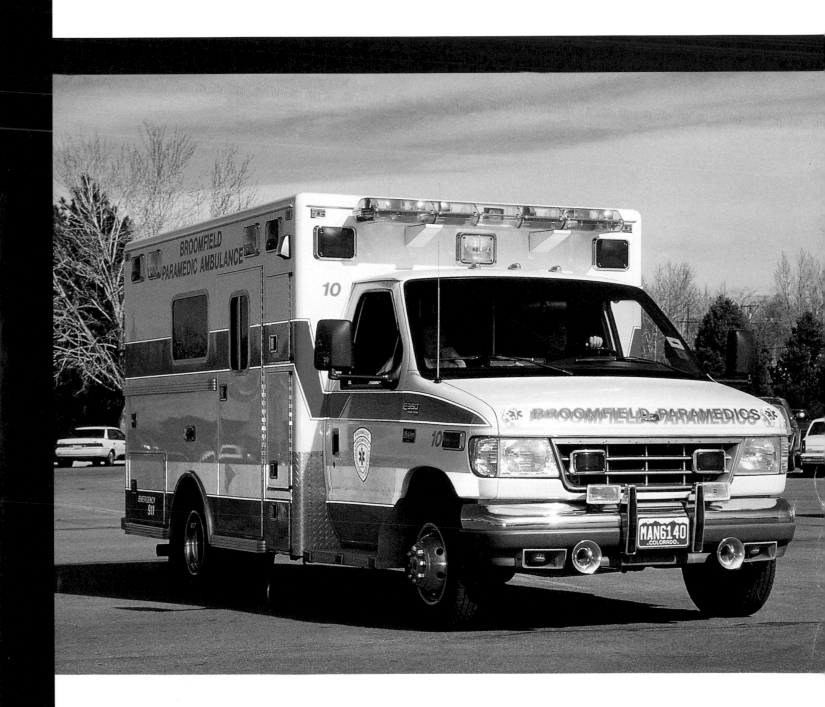

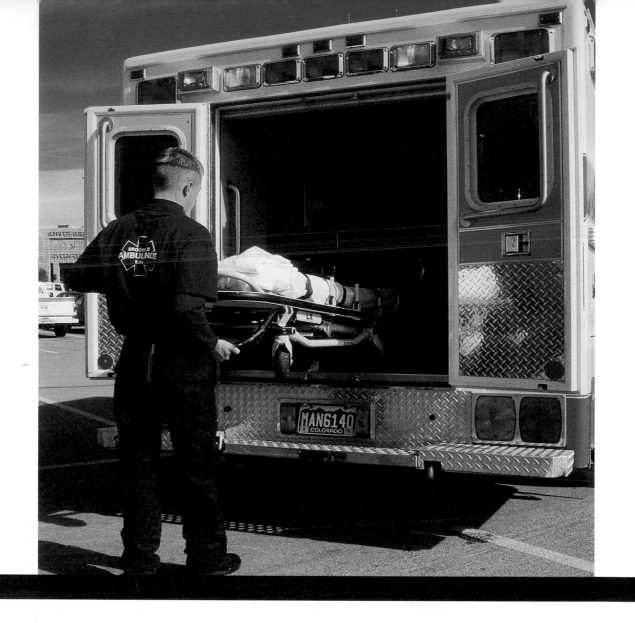

There is a small **cabin** in the back of the
ambulance. There is a **stretcher** in the
cabin. The **patient** lies on the stretcher.

A special worker called a **paramedic** rides with the patient. He or she gives the patient **first aid.**

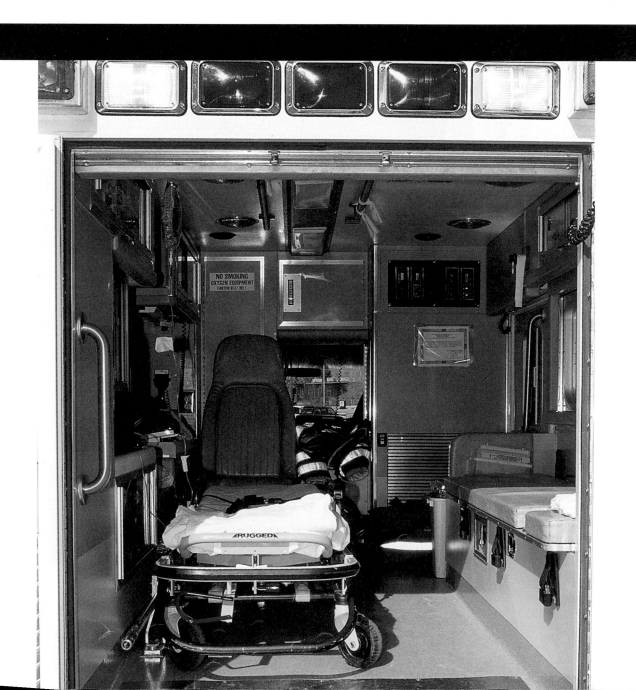

There are many **bins** in the ambulance.

The paramedic keeps many important

things inside the bins.

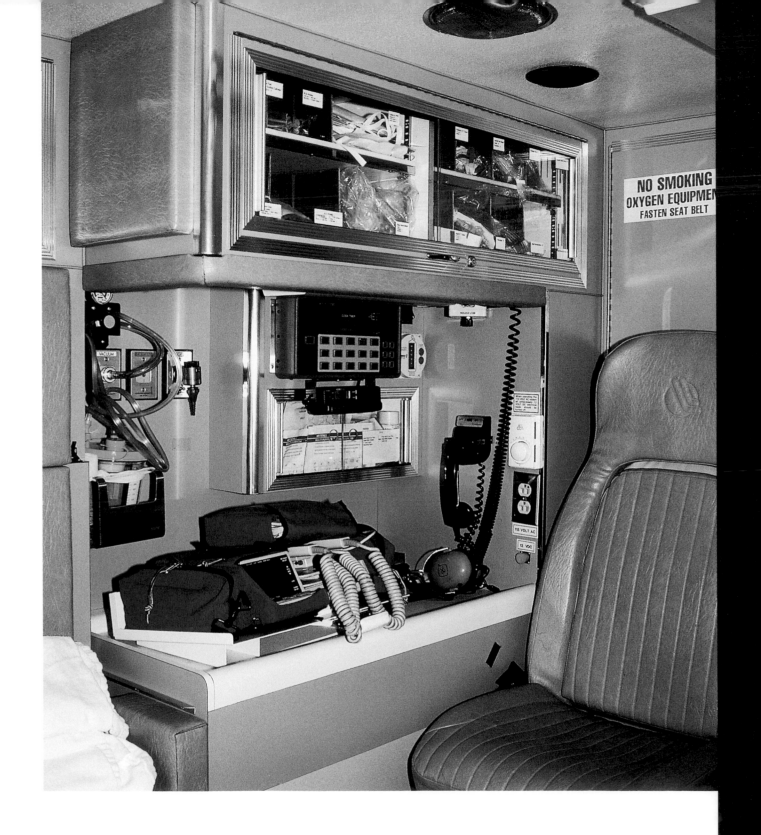

NO SMOKING
OXYGEN EQUIPMEN
FASTEN SEAT BELT

There are bins inside the cabin, too. The

paramedic stores first aid tools in these

bins. There is also a special telephone.

The paramedic can talk to doctors at the

hospital using the telephone.

An ambulance has bright, flashing
lights. It also has **sirens** that make
loud noises.

The lights and sirens warn other drivers. All drivers must move out of the way.

The ambulance driver turns on the sirens and lights. He uses **controls.** The siren can make different noises. The driver pushes a button to choose which noise he wants.

Climb Aboard!

Would you like to see where the driver sits? The ambulance driver is also a paramedic. He sits in the **cab.** He turns on the sirens and the lights. He uses a **radio** to talk to people at the hospital.

The inside of the cabin

1. The bins

2. The telephone

3. The first aid equipment

4. The stretcher

The inside of the cab

1. The radio

2. The siren and light controls

3. The steering wheel

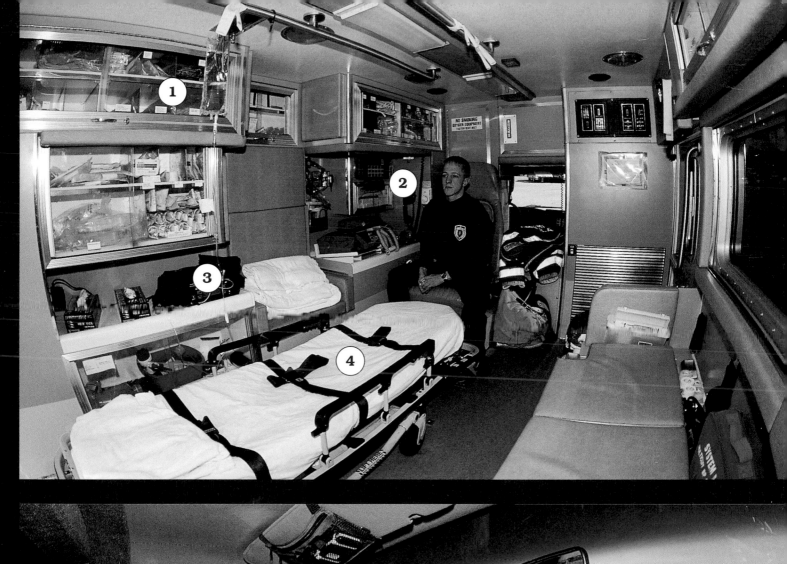

The outside

1. The side door

2. The lights

3. The sirens

4. The bins

5. The back door

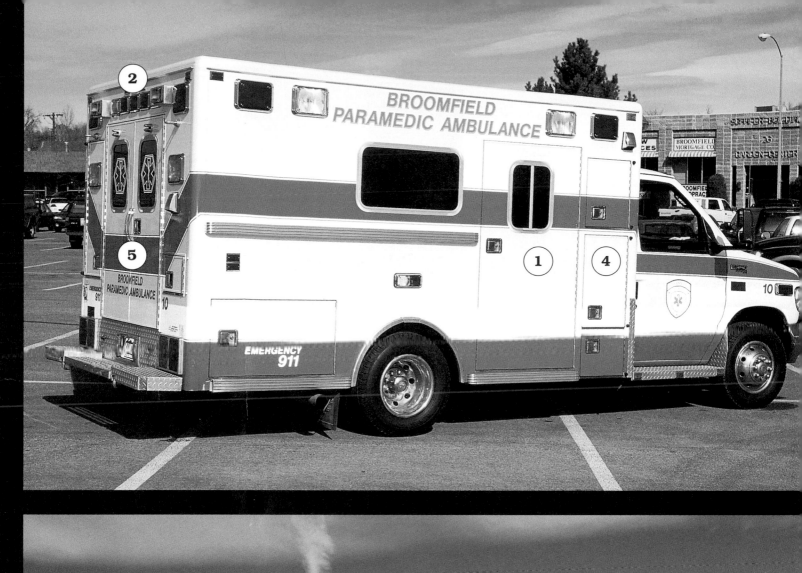

Glossary

bins (BINZ)
Bins are boxes inside the ambulance. The paramedic stores many things inside the bins.

cab (KAB)
A cab is the place where the ambulance's driver sits. The cab has a seat, a steering wheel, controls, and a radio.

cabin (KAB-en)
A cabin is the space inside an ambulance where patients sit. A paramedic also rides in the cabin.

controls (kun-TROLZ)
Controls are tools used to help make something work. An ambulance driver uses controls to turn on the sirens and lights.

equipment (ee-KWIP-mint)
Equipment is tools that people need to do their jobs. The paramedic uses medical equipment to care for patients.

first aid (FERST AYD)
First aid is care given to sick or injured people before they see a doctor. A paramedic gives patients first aid.

paramedic (par-uh-MED-ik)
A paramedic is a worker who is trained to work with injured and sick people. Paramedics take care of patients in an ambulance before they get to the hospital.

patient (PAY-shunt)
A patient is someone who needs medical care. Doctors and paramedics take care of patients.

radio (RAYD-ee-o)
A radio is a special machine on an ambulance. Paramedics use a radio to talk to people at the hospital or at the station.

sirens (SY-wrenz)
Sirens are horns that make very loud noises. An ambulance has sirens to warn people it is coming.

stretcher (STRECH-ur)
A stretcher is a moveable bed used to carry a sick or injured person. Paramedics put patients on stretchers.